Material Matters

Chemical Reactions

EXPRESS EDITION

Carol Baldwin

www.raintreepublishers.co.uk
Visit our website to find out more information about **Raintree** books.

To order:
☎ Phone 44 (0) 1865 888113
▤ Send a fax to 44 (0) 1865 314091
▢ Visit the Raintree Bookshop at **www.raintreepublishers.co.uk** to browse our catalogue and order online.

First published in Great Britain by Raintree Publishers, Halley Court, Jordan Hill, Oxford, OX2 8EJ, part of Harcourt Education Ltd.
Raintree is a registered trademark of Harcourt Education Ltd.

Produced for Raintree Publishers by Discovery Books Ltd.
Editorial: Louise Galpine, Carol Usher, Charlotte Guillain, and Isabel Thomas
Design: Victoria Bevan, Keith Williams (sprout.uk.com Limited), and Michelle Lisseter
Picture Research: Maria Joannou and Alison Prior
Production: Jonathan Smith and Duncan Gilbert
Originated by Dot Gradations Ltd
Printed and bound in China by South China Printing Company

ISBN 1 844 43358 7 (hardback)
09 08 07 06 05
10 9 8 7 6 5 4 3 2 1

ISBN 1 844 43621 7 (paperback)
09 08 07 06 05
10 9 8 7 6 5 4 3 2 1

British Library Cataloguing in Publication Data
Baldwin, Carol, 1943-
Chemical reactions. – (Freestyle express. Material matters)
1. Chemical reactions – Juvenile literature
541.3'9

A full catalogue record for this book is available from the British Library.

This levelled text is a version of
Freestyle: Material Matters: Chemical Reactions.

Photo acknowledgements
Page 33 right, Andrew Lambert; 13, Chris Honeywell; 39, Gareth Boden; 27, Trevor Clifford; 4, 20, 35, 41 Tudor Photography; 9 right, Art Directors & Trip; 14, Art Directors & Trip; 38, Art Directors & Trip; 40 right, Art Directors & Trip/ T Freeman; 42, Art Directors & Trip/A Lambert; 37, Art Directors & Trip/Australia Picture Library; 31, Art Directors & Trip/C Kapolka; 17, Art Directors & Trip/C Smedley; 24 right, Associated Press; 32, Associated Press; 4–5, 8, 15, 25, 36-37, 40 left, Corbis; Corbis; 10–11, Corbis/C O'Rear; 16, Corbis/Duomo; 28, Corbis/E Whiting; 22, Corbis/ G Rowell; 23, Corbis/MacFadden Publishing; 12–13, Corbis/O Franken; 22–23, Corbis/P Turnley; 28–29, Corbis/R Gehman; 10, Corbis/R Krist; 11, Corbis/T Lang; 43, Corbis/T Stewart; 18, Digital Vision; 34–35, FLPA/ Gerard Lacz; 14–15, FLPA/L Lewis; 20–21, FLPA/R Tidman; 19, FLPA/W Meinderts; 12, Foodpix; 5 bottom, Forensic Alliance; 42–43, Forensic Alliance; 5 top, 18-19, NASA/ Kennedy Space Centre; 29, NASA/Jet Propulsion Laboratory; 6–7, Photodisc; 7, Photodisc; 6, Robert Harding; 30, Science Photo Library/ Charles D Winters; 30–31, Science Photo Library/ Charles D Winters; 38–39, Science Photo Library/ Michael Abbey; 9 left, Science Photo Library/Alex Bartel; 21, Science Photo Library/CNRI; 26, Science Photo Library/D Parker; 26–27, Science Photo Library/D Spears; 24 left, Science Photo Library/M Chillmaid; 34, Science Photo Library/P Ryan/Scripps; 16–17, Science Photo Library/P Scoones; 5 middle, 36, 45 T.Waltham/Geophotos; 33 left, 44 TDG Nexus/Mark Perry/Simon Peachey.

Cover photograph of a reaction taking place in a test tube reproduced with permission of Corbis/ Lester Lefkowitz.

Every effort has been made to contact copyright holders of any material reproduced in this book. Any omissions will be rectified in subsequent printings if notice is given to the Publishers.

Disclaimer
All the Internet addresses (URLs) given in this book were valid at the time of going to press. However, due to the dynamic nature of the Internet, some addresses may have changed, or sites may have changed or ceased to exist since publication. While the author and Publishers regret any inconvenience this may cause readers, no responsibility for any such changes can be accepted by either the author or the Publishers.

Contents

Any words appearing in the text in bold, **like this**, are explained in the Glossary. You can also look out for some of them in the Word bank at the bottom of each page.

Explosion!

Different colours

The sparks in fireworks shoot out in all sorts of colours. These come from different chemicals. Yellow sparks come from sodium. A bright, white colour comes from magnesium. Green sparks come from copper.

A firework shoots high into the sky. Boom! The firework explodes. A splash of red spreads across the sky. A few seconds later another firework goes off. A huge ball of bright white sparks lights up the sky. Next there are sizzling, spinning wheels of green. Lights, colours, and sounds are all part of firework displays. They show that changes are taking place in the fireworks.

Fireworks contain explosive chemicals. They are very dangerous.

Changes all around us

Materials around us change all the time. Some changes take less than a second. Exploding fireworks are like this. Other changes take longer. The rusting of a car takes many years.

When materials change they often produce one or more new materials. If this happens a **chemical reaction** has taken place. This book tells you all about chemical reactions.

Fireworks give brilliant displays of light and noise. They are a big part in celebrations around the world.

Find out later ...

... how chemical reactions power the Space Shuttle.

... how caves form.

... how police use chemical reactions.

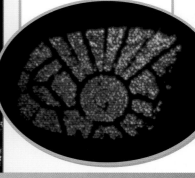

chemical reaction change that produces one or more new materials

Matter

Everything around us is made up of **matter**. The food we eat and the clothes we wear are matter. All matter is made up of **atoms**. Atoms are tiny **particles** that make up everything. But not all atoms are alike.

Elements

There are over a hundred **elements**. An element is made from just one kind of atom. Different elements are made from different atoms. Silver is an element. So are carbon and oxygen.

What is matter?
This flash of lightning is not matter. It is electrical **energy**. But the air it passes through is matter.

Water is a compound. It is made of the elements hydrogen and oxygen.

Word bank   matter anything that takes up space and has mass

Compounds

Compounds are made up of atoms of more than one element. Carbon dioxide is a compound. It is made of carbon and oxygen atoms. There is a set number of each kind of atom in a compound. Carbon dioxide has two oxygen atoms for each carbon atom.

The atoms in a compound join together in special ways. They are held together tightly. You can break compounds into simpler materials. But this is often hard to do.

Mixtures

The topping on this pizza is a **mixture**. It contains sauce, cheese, and other toppings. But they are not joined together. They can be separated quite easily.

mixture material made of elements or compounds not joined chemically

You can describe **matter** by its features. These are called **properties**. There are two main types of property. One kind is physical. The other kind is chemical.

Physical properties

You can find out the **physical properties** of a material easily. You do not need to change it. You can usually tell physical properties by looking or measuring. Colour and **state of matter** are physical properties. For example, lemon juice is yellow. It is in a liquid state. These are all physical properties.

Cars are different sizes, shapes, and colours. These are physical properties of cars.

state of matter whether a substance is solid, liquid or gas

Chemical properties

Chemical properties tell us how a material will **react** with something else. Wood is able to burn in air. This is a chemical property. It is useful because it gives us heat and light.

If you leave your bicycle outdoors it will rust in time. Rust forms when iron reacts with oxygen and water vapour in the air. This is a chemical property of iron. A material has to change before you can find out its chemical properties.

Coloured bottles

Vitamins usually come in dark bottles. This is to stop the light getting in. Most vitamins change in light. This is a chemical property.

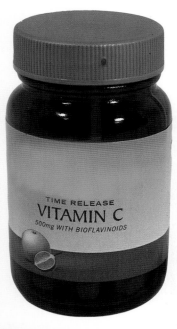

This is a pile of scrap material. The iron is attracted to this huge magnet. This is a useful physical property for separating iron.

Changing matter

A large bell
To make a bell, melted metal is poured into a mould. The metal then sets into a solid. A large bell must be cooled very slowly to prevent the metal cracking.

Physical changes
An artist carves wood to make a sculpture. He changes its shape, but he does not change the wood. This is a **physical change**.

Matter changes from solid to liquid, from liquid to gas, and back again. These are changes in **state of matter**. When liquid water changes to solid ice in a freezer it is still water. This is a physical change.

This is melted copper. When it cools it will turn back to a solid. This is a physical change.

The Liberty Bell, in Philadelphia, USA, cracked and had to be recast twice.

physical change change in how something looks, not in what makes it up

Chemical changes

When wood burns in a fireplace, it changes. The wood joins with oxygen in the air. Ash, **water vapour**, and carbon dioxide gas are formed. Ash is a soft, grey material. Water vapour and carbon dioxide are gases with no smell or colour. These new materials look and act differently from the wood. A chemical change, or a **chemical reaction**, has taken place.

A chemical reaction is a change which happens when new materials are formed.

Torch batteries

There are chemical changes going on in this torch's battery. These changes make electricity and light up the bulb.

chemical reaction change that produces one or more new materials

Baking cakes

When you bake a cake a chemical reaction happens. The ingredients **react** together. They make carbon dioxide gas. As the cake bakes, bubbles of carbon dioxide rise through the cake mix.

Clues to chemical changes

A **chemical reaction** is taking place if there is a fire. Other chemical changes give off **energy** without fire. The energy can be heat, light, sound, or electricity. Giving off energy is a sign of chemical change.

Sometimes gas forms when a chemical reaction takes place. You can see the bubbles of gas in the liquid. A colour change is another clue that there has been a chemical reaction. Sometimes when you put two clear liquids together they form a solid. The solid makes the liquid go cloudy.

This pancake has bubbles in its surface. They are a clue that a chemical reaction has taken place.

Gases escape into the air when wood burns. So burning wood gets lighter.

Word bank   energy ability to do work. Energy is transferred whenever something happens.

Keeping mass

When a chemical reaction takes place, new materials are formed. But the **mass** stays the same. The mass of something is the amount of **matter** it has. There are still the same number of **atoms**. The atoms are just rearranged.

In chemical reactions, no matter is lost and none is made. For example, iron and oxygen join together to form iron oxide. If you add the mass of the iron to the mass of the oxygen, you find that it is the same as the mass of the iron oxide.

Burning candles

A candle gets smaller as it burns. It looks as if it loses mass. But as it burns it gives off gases. The mass of the gases would be the same as the mass of the missing candle.

This candle needs oxygen to burn. Burning is a chemical reaction.

Describing chemical reactions

You can describe **chemical reactions** by using **word equations**. In a word equation the names of the **reactants** are on the left. The names of the **products** are on the right. An arrow separates these names. It means 'produces'. The arrow points from the reactants to the products.

Hydrogen **reacts** with oxygen to form water. The word equation for this reaction is:

$$\text{hydrogen} + \text{oxygen} \rightarrow \text{water}$$

The copper of this statue reacts with carbon dioxide and **water vapour** in the air. It forms a layer of green copper carbonate.

reactant material that reacts with another material during a chemical reaction

Chemical symbols

There is a short way of writing the names of **elements**. We use **chemical symbols**. Symbols can be one or two letters. The first letter is always a capital letter. The second letter is always lower case. For example the symbol for magnesium is Mg, not MG, and the symbol for sodium is Na, not NA.

Common chemical symbols

- Hydrogen   H
- Gold   Au
- Sodium   Na
- Copper   Cu
- Iron   Fe
- Sulphur   S
- Carbon   C

This is table salt or sodium chloride. It is a very safe **compound**. But it is made from sodium and chlorine. These are both dangerous **elements**.

product material formed from a chemical reaction

Chemical formulas

You can use **chemical symbols** to write **formulas**. A formula shows how **atoms** are joined and how many. Oxygen has the formula O_2. The O stands for oxygen. The '2' is written below the line. This tells us that there are two **atoms** of oxygen joined together.

Often a number is written on the line. Then it refers to atoms or **molecules** that are not joined. Two atoms of carbon that are not joined are written as 2C.

Formulas of compounds

Formulas are used to write the names of **compounds** too. The formula for carbon dioxide is CO_2. This means that a carbon dioxide molecule has one carbon atom and two oxygen atoms.

Chlorine

Chlorine **reacts** with most other **elements**. When hot sodium is put into a jar of chlorine gas, sodium chloride is formed. There is so much heat the sodium burns in the chlorine.

Chlorine is added to swimming pools. It kills bacteria.

formula symbols and numbers used to show how atoms are joined

The formula for water is H_2O. This means a molecule of water has two hydrogen atoms joined to one oxygen atom.

Aluminium is used to make these aeroplane wings.

This is a welding torch. It is being used under water. It uses the reaction between hydrogen, H_2, and oxygen, O_2, to produce extreme heat.

Aluminium
There is a lot of aluminium in the Earth's crust. But it is mostly found as aluminium **oxide**. A lot of energy is needed to produce pure aluminium. This makes it expensive.

molecule two or more atoms held together by chemical bonds

Kinds of chemical reaction

'Putting together' reactions

Often two or more **elements** or **compounds** join together. They form one new compound. This type of reaction is called a **synthesis reaction**. In synthesis reactions there is only one **product**. The reaction between iron and sulphur is like this. They join together to form the compound iron sulphide.

'Breaking apart' reactions

In some reactions a compound is broken apart. Then simpler materials are made. This type of reaction is called a **decomposition reaction**. A compound can break apart to form two elements. Water is made up of two hydrogen atoms and one oxygen atom. When water is split, hydrogen and oxygen are formed.

Acid in the air

Coal burning power stations produce sulphur oxides. These join with water in the air, forming **acids**. The acids fall to the Earth as **acid rain** or snow.

Acid rain flows into streams or ponds. There it can kill plants, frogs, fish, and snails.

Word bank   acid rain rain containing nitric acid and sulphuric acid

A single compound can break up into two other compounds. The **formula** for copper carbonate is $CuCO_3$. When copper carbonate is heated it breaks apart. It forms copper **oxide**, CuO, and carbon dioxide, CO_2. There is only one **reactant** in this reaction.

Decomposers
Some living things are called **decomposers**. Moulds and mushrooms are examples of these. They break apart the compounds in dead plants, animals, and waste. The simpler materials can be used again.

This beefsteak fungus gets **energy** by breaking down compounds in plant waste.

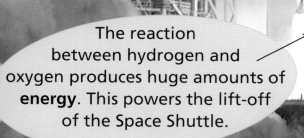

The reaction between hydrogen and oxygen produces huge amounts of **energy**. This powers the lift-off of the Space Shuttle.

decomposer living thing that breaks apart compounds into simpler materials

Button batteries

Button batteries are small. They are used to power watches and hearing aids. A displacement reaction takes place in button batteries. This releases the **energy**.

Displacement reactions

In this type of reaction you have one **element** on its own and a **compound**. The element pushes out one of the elements in the compound. It takes its place. This is a simple **displacement reaction**.

A simple displacement reaction is set up to make iron. Much of our iron comes from iron **oxide**. Ironworkers react iron oxide with carbon. The carbon 'pushes out' the oxygen, making carbon dioxide. This leaves iron on its own.

Large ships, like this, have magnesium bars in their iron hulls. The magnesium stops the iron hull from rusting in the salt water. This happens because of a displacement reaction.

OCEAN PRINCESS
NASSAU

Other displacement reactions

Displacement reactions can happen between two compounds. The elements in the two compounds switch places.

This happens when sodium chloride reacts with silver nitrate. First both compounds are **dissolved** in water. When they are mixed a white solid appears. This is silver chloride. Sodium nitrate is also formed. But that stays dissolved in the water. So you cannot see it. Sodium chloride and silver nitrate have 'swapped partners'. In this displacement reaction sodium nitrate and silver chloride are formed.

Looking inside
Barium sulphate shows up in X-rays. An ill person is given a barium sulphate **mixture** to drink. X-ray photographs are taken. They show doctors what the **intestine** looks like.

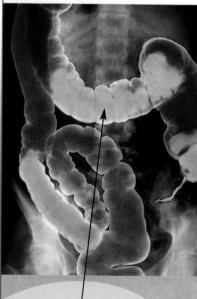

Barium sulphate is a solid. It is made in a displacement reaction.

Reactions and energy

Rusting

Rusting is an exothermic reaction. But if you touch a rusting car it does not feel hot. This is because rusting happens very slowly.

Exothermic reactions

When people go camping, they often light a fire. The wood gives off heat **energy** when it burns. It also gives off light energy. Many **chemical reactions** give off energy. They are called **exothermic reactions**. When something burns, it gives off heat and light energy. There is an exothermic reaction going on.

Some reactions give off heat and light energy slowly. They are still exothermic.

The iron in this car has reacted with water and oxygen in the air.

When a building catches fire, it can get so hot that the steel beams melt.

exothermic reaction reaction that gives off energy, usually in the form of heat and light

Endothermic reactions

Some chemical reactions need energy all the time to keep them going. As soon as there is no energy, they stop. They are called **endothermic reactions**. Carrots only cook when they are in hot water. If the carrots are put into cold water, they stop cooking.

We can split water into hydrogen and oxygen. But this reaction needs energy or it will stop. You have to pass electricity through the water. This process is called **electrolysis**.

In the limelight

Calcium oxide is often called **lime**. If lime gets very hot, it gives out a bluish-white light. This light was used to light theatre stages.

This stage is lit by electricity.

endothermic reaction reaction that takes in energy

Reaction rates

Fresh or sour

Keep milk cool. It stays fresh longer. Chemical reactions make milk sour. These happen more slowly at low temperatures.

This milk is sour. The liquid is called whey and the fatty solids are known as curds.

The grain, stored in these silos, has caught on fire. The dust from the grain burns so fast it can cause explosions.

Wood burns quickly and iron rusts slowly. These **chemical reactions** take different lengths of time. They have different rates. The **reaction rate** tells us how fast a reaction happens. There are two ways to measure the reaction rate. You can measure how quickly one of the **reactants** disappears. Or you can measure the time it takes for one of the **products** to form.

Temperature

Most chemical reactions speed up when the temperature increases. A cake will bake faster in a hot oven than in a cooler oven.

Concentration

The amount of a material in a certain space is the **concentration**. When the concentration is high, the **particles** are close together. They are more likely to bump into each other. A high concentration will speed up a reaction.

Particle size

Reactant particles can be different sizes. This affects the speed of a reaction. Smaller particles react faster. It is easier to start a fire with small twigs than big logs.

Flour bomb

Flour particles are very tiny. They have a huge **surface area**. They are more likely to touch each other. This means they burn instantly.

An explosion at this flour mill, in London, killed four people in 1965.

Catalysts

Chemical reactions can be too slow to be useful. Then people use **catalysts**. These speed up reactions. But catalysts do not take part in reactions. Catalysts do not change or get used up. The amount of catalyst at the end of the reaction is the same as at the start.

Seeing clearly

Contact lens cleaning solution contains enzymes. They work as a catalyst. It speeds up the reactions that break down the dirt. People can rinse the dirt off the lenses.

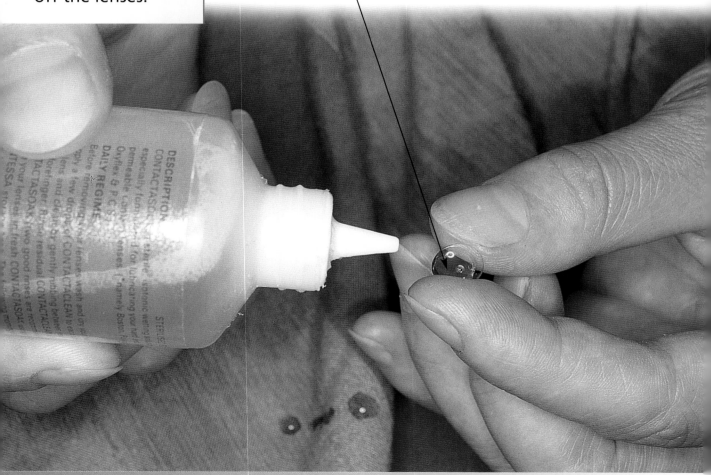

Dirt collects on contact lenses and they go cloudy. People need to clean them.

catalyst material that speeds up a reaction without being used up

Enzymes

All living things use catalysts. These are called **enzymes**. Spiders eat insects for food. First the spider bites the insect. Then it pours enzymes into the insect's body. The enzymes speed up the breakdown of the insect's body. It turns into soft goo and the spider sucks it up.

Inhibitors

Sometimes foods and medicines can go off too quickly. This is because chemical reactions happen too fast. They need to be slowed down. People use **inhibitors** to do this.

Browning apples

Chopped apple will react with oxygen in the air. This makes them turn brown. You can add lemon juice to the apples as soon as they are cut. This slows down or inhibits this reaction.

This spider is using enzymes to help break down its victim's body.

---

enzyme substance that speeds up reactions in living things without being changed

27

Some chemical reactions

Oxidation

Many materials **react** with oxygen. This is called **oxidation**.

Fast reactions with oxygen

Materials can react with oxygen very quickly. This is called burning. Paper, candles, and logs all burn because they react with oxygen fast.

Burning is useful. It gives off heat and light **energy**. We burn **fuel** to heat our homes and to run cars. Burning can also be harmful — fires can kill.

Burning without oxygen

Carbon monoxide can kill you. It is a gas with no colour or smell. When fuel burns and there is not enough oxygen, carbon monoxide forms.

This stove uses wood as a fuel. This can produce carbon monoxide, if there is not enough oxygen.

Word bank   oxidation reaction when a material joins up with oxygen

Slow reactions with oxygen

Materials can also react with oxygen slowly. This is called slow oxidation. Rusting is slow oxidation. Rust forms slowly on iron and steel in cars and bridges. Rust is the **compound** iron **oxide**.

Reduction

Some reactions remove oxygen from a material. This is called **reduction**. Reduction is the opposite of oxidation. Reduction reactions are useful. They are used to get a pure metal like zinc from a metal oxide, such as zinc oxide.

Rusty rocks
Some rocks have iron in them. The iron in them reacts with the oxygen in air. Iron oxide or rust forms. The rocks become red or orange in colour.

Forest fires kill plants and animals.

reduction reaction where oxygen is removed from a material

Reactivity series

Potassium
Sodium
Lithium
Calcium
Magnesium
Aluminium
Zinc
Iron
Tin
Lead
(Hydrogen)
Copper
Mercury
Silver
Gold
Platinum

more reactive

less reactive

Metals and water

Most metals do not **react** with water. But there are some metals that react violently. These are lithium, sodium, potassium, rubidium, and caesium. Other metals will react with water, but more slowly. These are calcium, strontium, and barium. Magnesium reacts very slowly with cold water.

Metals and acids

Only some metals react with **acids**. The **reactivity series** chart, on the left, tells us the metals that will do this. The metals listed above hydrogen react with acid. The metals listed below hydrogen do not react with acid.

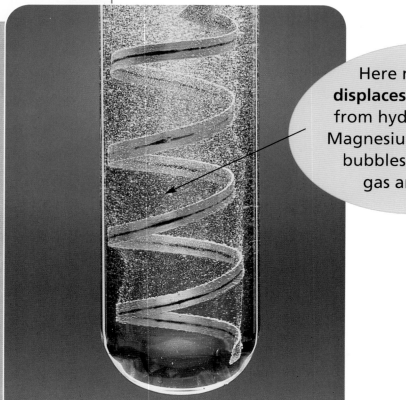

Here magnesium **displaces** the hydrogen from hydrochloric acid. Magnesium chloride and bubbles of hydrogen gas are formed.

reactivity series materials listed by how easily they react with other materials

Metals and other compounds

Some metals push out other metals in a **compound** during a **chemical reaction**. You can use the chart, opposite, to tell you the metals that will do this.

For example in the reaction between iron and copper sulphate, the iron pushes out the copper. Iron sulphate and copper are formed. This is because iron is more reactive than copper.

This potassium is reacting violently with water. Potassium must be stored under oil to keep it away from water.

Mending tracks

Aluminium reacts with iron oxide. The **products** are aluminium oxide and iron. This reaction produces huge amounts of heat. This melts the iron. The melted iron is used to mend rail tracks.

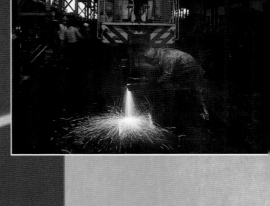

displace push out

31

Neutralization reactions

An **acid** will **react** with a **base**. Acids and bases cancel each other out. They form **neutral** materials. A neutral material is not an acid and it is not a base. Water is a neutral material.

The reaction between an acid and a base is called **neutralization**. This type of reaction forms water and a **salt**. This is shown below.

acid + base ⟶ salt + water

For example hydrochloric acid reacts with the base, sodium **hydroxide**. Water and the salt, sodium chloride, form.

Acid everywhere

In 1996 a train came off the rails. It was carrying a strong acid. The acid spilled across a motorway. This was in Colorado, USA. They used **soda ash** and **lime** to clean up the spill. These bases neutralized the acid.

Special suits protect people who clean up acid spills.

base chemical that neutralizes acids; metal oxides and metal hydroxides are bases

Salts

Sodium chloride is the **compound** we call salt. Sodium chloride is used to make many things. These include ice cream, rubber, and soap. But this is just one of many salts.

A salt is made when an acid reacts with a base. Nitric acid reacts with potassium hydroxide. The salt potassium nitrate is formed. This salt is used to make **fertilizers** and explosives.

Other acid reactions

Limestone, marble, and chalk are forms of calcium **carbonate**. Carbonates react with acids. They produce bubbles of carbon dioxide gas.

This tanker is carrying sodium hydroxide. The numbers on the label tells us this. It also shows us the possible dangers.

2R
1824
CORROSIVE
8
SPECIALIST ADVICE 01928 580588
TDG NEXUS

Scientists use this acid reaction to test for carbonate rock.

carbonate compound that contains carbon, oxygen, and another element

Reactions in nature

Food without light

The deep parts of the sea are very dark. Sunlight cannot reach these depths. **Bacteria** make food using sulphur **compounds**. This happens where hot water spurts out of the sea floor.

Tube worms live in deep seas. They live on bacteria.

Eucalyptus trees make their own food. This koala has to eat the leaves to get energy.

respiration chemical reaction in which glucose and oxygen react to form carbon dioxide and water, releasing energy

Photosynthesis

Plants can make their own food. This happens in the green parts, such as leaves and some stems. This process is called **photosynthesis**. A green chemical in the leaves traps the Sun's light **energy**. Plants take in carbon dioxide gas through tiny pores in their leaves. The plant takes in water from the soil through its roots. Light energy from the Sun is used to **react** carbon dioxide and water together. A sugar, called **glucose**, and oxygen are produced.

Respiration

All living things need energy to grow and live. They use a process called **respiration**. This produces energy, when glucose and oxygen react. Plants make their own glucose. Animals eat plants and other animals to get glucose. Animals breathe in oxygen. Plants take in oxygen through the tiny pores in their leaves. Energy, carbon dioxide, and water are produced.

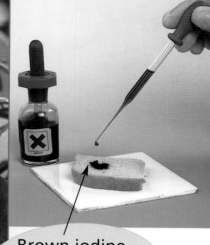

Brown iodine turns blue-black if starch is there.

Breaking down food

Foods, like bread, contain **starch**. Starch is made up of glucose. When we chew we make **saliva**. Saliva breaks down starch into glucose.

photosynthesis chemical reaction that uses light energy to react carbon dioxide with water. This produces glucose and oxygen.

Acids and carbonates

Carbonates are **compounds** that contain carbon and oxygen. **Acids react** with carbonates. This reaction produces a **salt**, water, and carbon dioxide gas. Caves form when an acid reacts with carbonate rocks.

How caves form

The reason caves form in the first place is rain. Rainwater joins with carbon dioxide in the air. It makes a weak acid, called carbonic acid. This acid reacts with calcium carbonate rocks, like limestone. Caves and tunnels are made as the acid eats through the rock.

Lechuguilla Cave

This cave is in New Mexico. It formed when acid ate through the limestone underground.

Lechuguilla Cave is a maze of tunnels and caves.

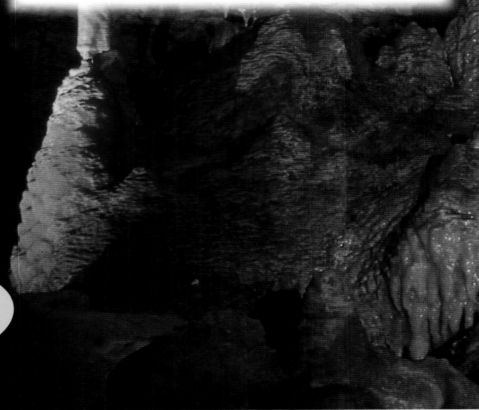

Acid rain

Burning **fossil fuels**, like coal, gas, and oil, causes **acid rain**. Sulphur dioxide and nitrogen oxide gases combine with the **water vapour** in the air. This forms strong acids. These acids fall to the Earth in rain and snow.

Acid rain reacts with marble and limestone. This damages many buildings and statues. Acid rain kills some kinds of tree. It also makes soils acidic and some plants cannot grow in them.

Neutralizing acidic lakes

Most living things die in acidic water. But you can treat it with powdered limestone. This **neutralizes** the acid in the water. Then plants and animals can live in the water again.

Aeroplanes, helicopters, and boats are used to spread limestone on acidic lakes.

fossil fuel fuel formed from the remains of plants and animals that lived millions of years ago; coal, oil, and gas are fossil fuels

Amazing reactions

Non-stick cookware

Cooking eggs is easy in this frying pan. It has a non-stick surface. The slippery substance used on the surface was found by accident. This was a surprise chemical reaction!

Baking bread

To make bread 'rise' people mix **yeast** into bread dough. Yeast **reacts** with the sugar in wheat flour. The reaction forms carbon dioxide gas and alcohol. The gas makes many little bubbles. These cause the bread dough to rise.

The heat from the oven drives off the carbon dioxide and the alcohol. But tiny holes are left through the bread. This is where the carbon dioxide gas bubbles were formed.

This photo is of tiny yeast cells. It was taken through a microscope.

Word bank   yeast type of fungus used to make bread rise

Body enzymes

Our bodies need food for growth and repair. But food has to be broken down into simple chemicals. Then our bodies can use it. This process is called **digestion**.

Digestion is a whole series of **chemical reactions**. **Enzymes** speed up the chemical reactions. Food is broken down in the mouth, the stomach, and the small intestine.

Lactose intolerance

Some people do not have the enzyme lactase. Lactase breaks down lactose. Lactose is the type of sugar found in milk.

Milk shakes like these make some people ill.

---

digestion breakdown of food, so that it can be used by the body

Using hand warmers

Hand warmers are small pouches. They contain iron powder and **catalysts**. When you shake the pouch, it mixes the iron powder with air. The iron powder **reacts** with oxygen in the air to form rust. This reaction gives off heat. The catalysts speed up the reaction. This means heat is given off much faster than normal rusting.

Reactions in your mouth

Bacteria in our mouths produce **acids**. The acid reacts with the surface of the teeth. Then bacteria and acid attack the inside of the teeth too.

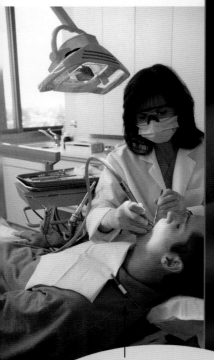

Brush your teeth and see a dentist often! This keeps teeth free of acid-producing bacteria.

Campers and scuba divers use lightsticks. They are also used for decoration and fun.

Word bank catalyst substance that speeds up a reaction without being used up

Using lightsticks

When you bend a lightstick the chemicals inside mix. As soon as the chemicals touch each other they react. The reaction is **exothermic**. It produces light **energy**. This causes the lightstick to glow.

In the cold the reaction is slower. The lightstick glows less, but lasts longer. In the warm the reaction is faster. The lightstick glows brighter but for a shorter time.

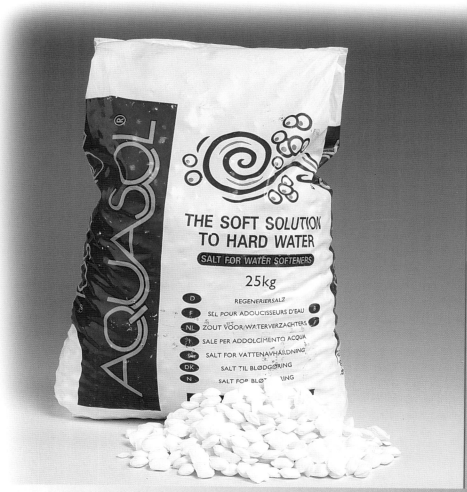

Hard water
Water is 'hard' because it has **salts dissolved** in it. The salts react with soap to form soap scum. Soap scum sticks to the sides of baths.

bacteria living things, so small you need a microscope to see them

Hospital science

Doctors use chemical tests. These find out why a person is ill. The tests measure chemicals in the blood. One test measures how much **glucose** is in the blood. If the glucose level is high, a person might have **diabetes**.

There are many other tests to check a person's health. They all depend on **chemical reactions**.

Daily blood tests

People with diabetes have to check the glucose in their blood. The tests they use are all reactions between glucose and other chemicals.

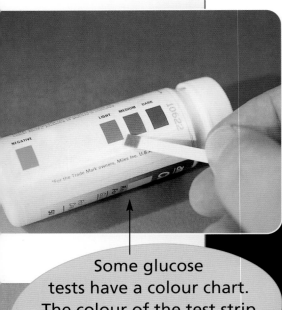

Some glucose tests have a colour chart. The colour of the test strip shows the person's glucose level.

glucose compound that is a type of sugar

Forensic science

Police use chemical tests to help solve crimes. Luminol is one chemical police use. This helps them look for traces of blood. Police mix luminol with hydrogen peroxide. Normally this produces a very slow **exothermic** reaction. In the dark the police would see a faint blue-green glow in time.

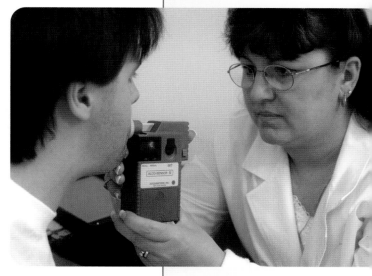

But if blood is there, the reaction happens much quicker. The police see a bright glow in seconds.

Take a deep breath and blow
Police used to ask drivers to breathe into a bag if they thought the driver had been drinking alcohol. The bag contained a red-orange chemical. This **reacts** with alcohol and turns green.

Luminol still glows if the blood is very old. It works even if the area has been cleaned.

Find out more

Websites

BBC Science
News, features, and activities on science.
www.bbc.co.uk

Creative Chemistry
Fun, practical activities, quizzes, puzzles, and more.
www.creative-chemistry.org.uk

Skoool.co.uk
Help for science projects and homework.
http://kent.skoool.co.uk

Books
Chemicals in Action: Material Changes and Reactions, Chris Oxlade (Heinemann Library, 2002)
Material World: Changing Materials, Robert Snedden (Heinemann Library, 2001)
Matter, Ann Fullick (Heinemann Library, 1999)

World Wide Web
To find out more about chemical reactions you can search the Internet. Use keywords like these:
- fireworks
- crime +science
- reactions +catalysts
- chemicals +reactions

You can find your own keywords by using words from this book. The search tips on the next page will help you find useful websites.

Search tips

There are billions of pages on the Internet. It can be difficult to find exactly what you are looking for. These tips will help you find useful websites more quickly:

- Know what you want to find out about

- Use simple keywords

- Use two to six keywords in a search

- Only use names of people, places or things

- Put double quote marks around words that go together, for example "neutralization reactions"

Where to search

Search engine
A search engine looks through millions of website pages. It lists all the sites that match the words in the search box. You will find the best matches are at the top of the list, on the first page.

Search directory
A person instead of a computer has sorted a search directory. You can search by keyword or subject and browse through the different sites. It is like looking through books on a library shelf.

Glossary

acid compound that has a sour taste and can burn you. Acids have a pH less than 7.

acid rain rain containing nitric acid and sulphuric acid

atom tiny particle that makes up everything

bacteria living things, so small you need a microscope to see them

base chemical that neutralizes acids; metal oxides and metal hydroxides are bases

carbonate compound that contains carbon, oxygen, and another element

catalyst material that speeds up a reaction without being used up

chemical property how a material will react when it is with other materials

chemical reaction change that produces one or more new materials

chemical symbol short way of writing the name of an element

compound material made of two or more different types of atom

concentration amount of a material in a certain space

decomposer living thing that breaks apart compounds into simpler materials

decomposition reaction chemical reaction in which a compound breaks apart into simpler materials

diabetes condition in which there is too much sugar in the blood

digestion breakdown of food, so that it can be used by the body

displace push out

displacement reaction chemical reaction in which one or more elements displace, or push out, another in a compound

dissolve mix completely and evenly

electrolysis using electricity to break a compound apart

element material made from only one kind of atom

endothermic reaction reaction that takes in energy

energy ability to do work. Energy is transferred whenever something happens.

enzyme material that speeds up reactions in living things without being changed

exothermic reaction reaction that gives off energy, usually in the form of heat and light

fertilizer chemicals added to soils to help plants grow

formula symbols and numbers used to show how atoms are joined

fossil fuel fuel formed from the remains of plants and animals that lived millions of years ago; coal, oil, and gas are fossil fuels

fuel any material that can be burned to produce useful heat or power

glucose compound that is a type of sugar

hydroxide compound of a metal, hydrogen, and oxygen

inhibitor material that slows down a chemical reaction

intestine digestive canal between the stomach and the anus

lime calcium oxide or calcium hydroxide

mass amount of matter in an object

matter anything that takes up space and has mass

mixture material made of elements or compounds not joined chemically

molecule two or more atoms held together by chemical bonds

neutral neither an acid nor a base

neutralization reaction between an acid and a base to form a salt and water

oxidation reaction when a material joins up with oxygen

oxide compound formed when oxygen joins up with another element

particle tiny bit

photosynthesis chemical reaction that uses light energy to react carbon dioxide with water. This produces glucose and oxygen.

physical change change in how something looks, not in what makes it up

physical property feature that can be seen or measured without changing what a material is made of

product material formed from a chemical reaction

property feature of something

react take part in a chemical reaction and produce one or more new materials

reactant material that reacts with another material during a chemical reaction

reaction rate measure of how fast a reaction happens

reactivity series materials listed by how easily they react with other materials

reduction reaction where oxygen is removed from a material

respiration chemical reaction in which glucose and oxygen react to form carbon dioxide and water, releasing energy

saliva juice made in the mouth that contains an enzyme

salt material formed when an acid reacts with a base

soda ash sodium oxide

starch compound made of glucose units joined together

state of matter whether something is solid, liquid, or gas

surface area parts of a material that come in contact with a reactant

synthesis reaction chemical reaction in which two or more elements or compounds join to form one compound

vitamin chemical found in foods and needed for good health

water vapour water in a gas state

word equation chemical reaction described in words as an equation

yeast type of fungus used to make bread rise

Index

Titles in the Freestyle Express: Material Matters series include:

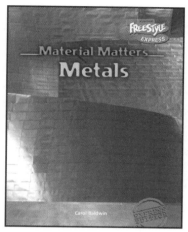

Hardback   1 844 43356 0

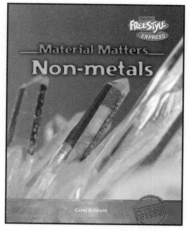

Hardback   1 844 43357 9

Hardback   1 844 43358 7

Hardback   1 844 43381 1

Hardback   1 844 43382 X

Hardback   1 844 43601 2

Find out about other Freestyle Express titles on our website www.raintreepublishers.co.uk